The first 8 days of being a mom

Translated and edited from the Netherlands by Gea Meijering

*How to take care of **you** as well as your newborn!*

This day-by-day manual includes:

* *Newborn care*
* *Maternal care and recovery*
* *'How to' pictures and illustrations*
* *Explanations in plain English*
* *Room to add special memories*

iCare PRESS

iCare Press LLC • www.thefirst8days.com

The first 8 days
of being a mom

How to take care of you as well as your newborn!

iCare Press LLC • www.icarepress.com

The first 8 days of being a mom. Translated, revised and updated from the Dutch original: Kraamwijzer; informatie over de bevalling en de dagen daarna, by Alle®zorg.

Published by:
iCare Press LLC
icarepress@gmail.com
www.icarepress.com

ISBN: 978-0-692-00009-0
17/01-1
For general information, sales inquiries and resellers information, contact iCare Press at icarepress@gmail.com or www.icarepress.com.

Special sales
This book is available at special discounts for bulk purchases. Special editions, including corporate imprints, can be created in large quantities for special needs. For more information please check www.icarepress.com, or e-mail icarepress@gmail.com.

Cover photography: Geranda Laros with special thanks to Yvanka and baby Sienna Betti.
Illustrations: Guusje Kaayk
Photography: Rob Stork with thanks to Ayzo van Betten, Mats van Hoeijen and parents.
Design cover and interior: Jan Schrieber

Contents

Introduction

There you are, in the middle of one of the most life changing events ever. You are going to have a baby and become a mother.

I gave birth to my first son in the Netherlands twenty months before I delivered my second son in a hospital in sunny California. I thought I was an experienced mother. I had done it before. But when I packed up my little bundle after two days in the hospital and headed home, I was unsure. I didn't remember much of anything from the first time anymore. What should I do in the next few days when my baby is crying? Is he hungry? Is he getting enough milk? How do I bathe him again? Where is the manual for this tiny little baby? And on top of that, I am still recovering from the delivery, my boobs are going to explode any second and I really can't find a comfortable sitting position. Is there something I can do to relieve the pressure? When is this going to stop? What should I do?

In the Netherlands where I gave birth to my first son, I had the luxury of having a specialized nurse at my house for the first 8 days. Every woman in the Netherlands has the opportunity to use this specialized care as insurance companies classify it under basic coverage.

The nurse is specialized in taking care of newborn babies and their mothers. She tells you everything you need to know, shows you how to do it, and checks on you as well as your baby. You can ask her a thousand questions and she takes care of other family members and your house. Isn't that fantastic? When we met her the first time to talk things through before the delivery, she brought the 'Kraamwijzer.' This is a book with information about the delivery and the days right after. I could read it before my delivery and she used it when helping me at home to record and explain things.

When I came home from the U.S. hospital with my second son, I didn't have a nurse or friends or anyone else that knew anything about newborns. I was terrified. So I grabbed my 'Kraamwijzer' and used it again as a reference guide. It was a great reassurance to read and to discover that what I was going through and doing was normal and that my instincts were generally right. I translated most of it in this book. I changed some things that are more common practice in the U.S. and I added a few others because, while it would be nice, most women in the U.S. are not afforded a bedside professional caregiver for the first 8 days to give them this kind of information.

For the most part, every woman with a newborn baby endures the same challenging new stages as any other woman anywhere in the world.

I hope this book will be helpful to you as you navigate through those first equally exciting and exhausting days.

Gea Meijering

Is this book for me?

This book is very useful for every woman who is going to have a baby!

Whether you deliver your baby in the hospital, at home, or in a birthing center, with either a vaginal delivery or with a Cesarean, it doesn't matter. Every new mother with a newborn baby can use the information in this book. It is also educational for fathers and other family members.

About this Book

This book gives you information relevant to a brand new mother and her newborn baby without a lot of theories or difficult terminology. I wanted to keep it as short and simple as can be. You don't have time to read 200+ pages when you've just had your baby. This book is not a statement for or against any type of delivery, place of delivery, type of feeding or any other choice in this precious event. Provided her medical condition allows, only the mother can decide what she wants and how. Honest, straightforward information about what matters is what can be found in these pages.

Whether you want reassurance, practical tips or to have it as a keepsake, it's all fine. Browse through it or read it chapter by chapter. You can use this whether you will be a first time mom or adding exponentially to your brood.

Conventions Used in This Book

In this book we are talking about the Ob-Gyn or family doctor, although in some cases a nurse or doula can take the place of the doctor for certain activities. Also we are talking about the Ob-Gyn and doctor as a 'she,' but of course that also can be a 'he.' For your reading convenience we are using the word 'he' when we are talking about the baby instead of constantly using he/she. In turn, 'she' is solely used for the mother. Logical isn't it?

Where Does All This Wisdom Come From?

The original Dutch version of this book was carefully put together by an editorial team consisting of the specialized nurse we talked about earlier, who takes care of the baby and mother at home, a children's nurse working in the hospital, a lactation specialist, a midwife (who takes care of the majority of the births in the Netherlands), and a pediatrician. All with years and years of hands on experience and knowledge. After translating, everything was first checked with existing information on the internet and parenting handbooks. Then a group of very nice dedicated, experienced specialists reviewed it and gave their input. This group consisted of three pediatricians, a midwife, doula and Ob-Gyn.

And on top of that all, everyone that worked on this book has experienced the wonder, excitement, and exhaustion of the first 8 days of being a mom first hand. What better source is there?

Nice Memories

Every 'Day' chapter features room to write something special about that day. This way you can read it back later and remember what happened during the very first days of your baby's life. It can also be a useful reflection tool should you decide to go for another baby.

Tell Us

We would like to hear from you. Your opinion matters to us. It matters to your fellow moms, too. And we'd like to hear it. In fact, we need to hear it.

When you share your experiences, tips and stories you actively help future moms. We will publish your experiences and discoveries directly on www.thefirst8days.com.

Your feedback about the book is of tremendous value to us. Give us your opinion instantly at our website www.thefirst8days.com or e-mail us at icarepress@gmail.com.

The Preparation

The due date is just a guide-line. A natural delivery gener-ally takes place between week 37 and week 42. You can al-most count on finally meeting your baby face to precious face within about three weeks of the due date. Having everything ready by that time will give you some extra peace of mind and keep you from having to pack everything in that hectic last minute.

For a delivery in the hospital you need:

Items for mom:
___ Toiletries (toothbrush, toothpaste, hair brush, deodorant, lotion)
___ 2 T-shirts or nightgowns (front-buttoning)
___ Slippers and warm socks
___ Bathrobe
___ Stretchy underwear or panties
___ Nursing bras
___ Breast pads
___ Clean, comfortable clothing
___ Cell phone
___ This book, of course!

Items for the baby:
___ Set of clothes for the baby
___ Onesies
___ Little pants, socks, and sweater
___ Jacket or babycape and hat
___ A safe baby car seat (check the internet for safety information on different types of car seats at www. www.safercar.gov/parents/

Items for the hospital personnel:
___ Insurance papers
___ Insurance card
___ Hospital admissions papers (most hospitals will let you file the paper-work a month or two before)
___ Birth plan
___ Your pediatrician's name and contact information

Items for your partner:
___ Your cell phone
___ List of phone numbers of family and friends
___ Photo camera, video camera, batteries, charger, earbuds
___ Snacks and drinks for your partner, and you if allowed
___ Money for parking
___ Books, magazines
___ Music

For a Delivery at Home:
If you are planning on giving birth at home, your midwife should provide you with a list of items to have on hand at least a month prior to your due date. You will also need many of the items listed under the hospital delivery preparation, so check those out, too.

You may also want to consider raising your bed if it is low to the ground, as this will relieve strain to your hips, knees and back. This is also better for any helpers you have at your bedside. People with sleigh and more traditional beds need not worry, but for those with a more contemporary design flair, you can buy bed platforms and frames at specialty stores. If you're in a pinch, crates will do just fine.

Birth Plan

Consider making a birth plan ahead of time. If you've established a close relationship with the Ob-Gyn who has cared for you at every appointment you may want to forgo a birth plan. But if your Ob-Gyn works in a group and you don't see the same doctor every time or if your Ob-Gyn will be unavailable for your delivery, consider making a birth plan. If you plan to deliver with a mid-wife the same things go, of course.

A birth plan is a list of all of the preferences and choices you want to share with everyone who will be present at your delivery. It can cover a wide variety of items such as:

- Labor, monitoring, Cesarean, episiotomy, delivery preferences

- Labor augmentation/induction

- Anesthesia/pain medication

- Immediate post-delivery actions and preferences

- Breastfeeding, circumcision preferences

- Photo/video preferences

- Environmental, food and beverage preferences

At time of the delivery you might not be able to point out exactly what you do and don't want. The birth plan is YOUR instruction to the delivery team.

As you start to consider all of the options, you might begin to feel over-whelmed however it's important to think about it and educate yourself before-hand, not when the pressure is on.

There are many ways to get more information on this very important subject. Check the internet to find more information, ask your doctor, midwife or doula, ask a friend who just had a baby or go to your local library for books on how to make a birth plan.

Tip:

You can prevent irritation of your baby's delicate skin by washing all new baby clothing, linens, etc. in advance with a hypo-allergenic, fragrance-free detergent, free of bleach and softeners. Dreft, Method for Baby, Seventh Generation Ultra Concentrated Baby Laundry detergent, The Honest Company, Meyers and Greenshield are merely a few of the current options.

Ultrasound picture made on:

(space for ultrasound picture)

day 1

After the longest nine months of your life, the big moment is finally here. This chapter explains what happens on the delivery day and will help you anticipate the processes that lie ahead of you.

The Signals

In the last weeks of pregnancy it is possible that you'll start to feel your uterus tighten up. While your belly may feel hard and sensitive, these Braxton Hicks contractions are simply the muscles of the uterus regularly pulling together and are generally not painful, though I know some moms who might not agree.

In these last days, even before the true contractions start, you might lose the 'mucus plug,' a thick, slimy plug of mucus that may have some blood on it. This means that the uterus is preparing to deliver. Sometimes it can even take a few days before the actual delivery begins. Also at the end of the pregnancy, your water bag can break spontaneously. Day or night. Sometimes in one dramatic big gush like in the movies or you just might feel a trickle unlike any you've felt before. As a precaution, you might want to protect your mattress with a plastic cover. The water smells a little bit sweet and should be transparent (colorless). Contact your doctor or midwife if you think your water has broken.

In most cases, the water breaks after contractions have started. Sometimes the water breaks first and then contractions start. If this does not happen you will probably be induced at the hospital. This is done to reduce the chance of infections.

Calling your Doctor or Midwife

Your doctor or midwife will give you guidelines for when to call should you have signs of starting delivery. Make notes of what you want to say when you call. You will be asked questions about the time between contractions, when they started, and other signals. They often listen to your voice to hear how you are doing and will decide, depending on what you say, when you should go to the hospital or when the midwife should come to your home.

The Delivery

Often a delivery starts with lower back pain or what feels like menstrual pain. Slowly it will become clear to you that the contractions have started. You'll recognize contractions because they start really softly, then take on in force fiercely and take off in force again. In between contractions you do not feel anything. You might get a little nervous: the big moment has started.

In the hospital you will be assigned a delivery nurse who will stay with you until you deliver. She will check all your vital signs and inform the doctor when necessary. She will assist you during the delivery when she can. Of course, the midwife does the same for you at home.

The First Stage of Labor

At the start, contractions will come and go easily. But gradually they will increase in tempo and strength. The cervix gradually dilates with the contractions. Once you are dilated to 10 centimeters, the baby can be born. This period of dilation will take the longest time, from a few hours up to even two days if it is your first delivery. The nurse, midwife or doctor will check on you regularly. In between contractions they can check how dilated you are.

The Second Stage of Labor

When dilation is complete, the passage is big enough for the baby to pass through. Birth will start. In this phase you will have fierce contractions. You will experience these as an enormous desire to push. It may feel like you do not have much control over your own body anymore, the urge to push is so strong. The nurse/doctor/midwife will accompany you through this birthing process. She will help you decide when it is a good time to push and when to

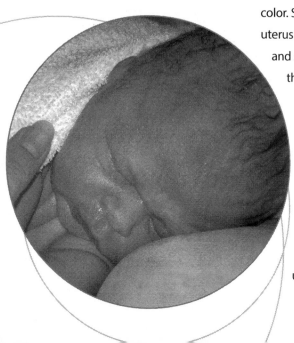

wait as well as how far along you are and what she sees. For first time mothers this phase can take two hours or more, but it can also go a lot quicker, especially for second babies. If the baby's head is in sight (a.k.a. crowning), you generally only have to push a couple more times until the baby is out.

The doctor or midwife will hold the baby, or maybe lay him on your stomach, while cleaning the baby's mouth and drying him. The doctor or midwife will clamp the umbilical cord and ask your partner if he wants to cut the cord.

The Third Stage of Labor

Shortly after the delivery you will have afterbirth contractions: the uterus contracts down and the placenta comes off the wall of the uterus. The nurse will ask you to push during a contraction. These contractions are less painful and you probably won't feel them much. The duration of the third stage varies from 10 minutes to a half an hour. During the delivery of the placenta as well as during the delivery, the nurse will check your blood loss and skin color. She will also monitor how fast the uterus is involuting (pulling together) and see if the placenta is intact. After the delivery of the placenta, the doctor or midwife will determine if you need sutures. Sutures may be administered with local anesthesia and if you have an epidural you are usually quite numb.

After the delivery, someone will check the firmness of your uterus and determine the extent

of blood loss. Usually you will be able to nurse the baby first. After that you are encouraged to go to the restroom. This way the uterus will pull together better and you will loose less blood. If you are dizzy, tell the nurse.

Sometimes based on the risk of hypertension/bleeding and due to numbness of the epidural, the nurse could empty the bladder.

Epidural for Pain Control

An epidural is one of the most effective methods of pain relief during a vaginal delivery. Its use has increased dramatically in the U.S. over the past 50 years. Some women use an epidural to help with pain control whereas other women do well naturally and do not require an epidural. While side effects and complications from epidurals are rare, there are certain risks involved. Every woman should consider the benefits and risks and apply them to their own circumstances.

A few of these risks include: rise of the mother's body temperature, drop in the mother's blood pressure, and procedural risks such as infection, bleeding and damage to surrounding nerves and organs.

Sometimes, for example in case of fetal distress, it is necessary to help nature a little bit by making a cut in the perineum called an episiotomy, allowing the baby to quicker enter into the world. Doctors might also recommend forceps or a vacuum to help the delivery along.

Every woman reacts differently to the delivery process. Some women become very emotional while others become very angry or short, even towards their partner. These are all parts of the process. They are normal and you don't have to be ashamed. Really. Some women tend to panic during the delivery. Even if you are well prepared, the pain can overwhelm you and you can become afraid. Watching your breathing can help as can doing some relaxing exercises with your partner.

How Does an Epidural Work?

You will be given regional anesthesia in the lower back that will numb your lower body as the epidural blocks pain from contractions while you are awake and alert. An anesthesiologist generally administers it.

Before giving you the injection, the doctor may numb your lower back with a local anesthetic. While you are sitting or lying on your side with your back curved, the doctor will insert the needle for the epidural. She will then pass a small flexible tube called a catheter through the needle. You will probably feel some pressure as the needle is inserted, but it is usually not painful. The needle is then removed, leaving the tube in place so you can receive more medication as needed. An epidural takes about 20 minutes to administer and about another 20 minutes to take effect.

Strategies for Getting Through Labor

There is no such thing as an easy delivery but by taking a childbirth education class you will learn a lot of things that will help you during labor and delivery.

The Bradley Method and Lamaze are two of the available educational options. The Bradley Method is a natural childbirth approach that involves pre-natal education, relaxation techniques, and partner participation. Lamaze focuses on similar points. The classes focus on the process of labor and birth as well as strategies for women and their partners to enhance the progress of labor while reducing pain and fear. Lamaze classes empower women to make informed choices about their delivery and allow them to put their faith and trust into their inner wisdom. The Bradley Method is usually given in 12 sessions and Lamaze is usually only one or two lessons.

Another option is HypnoBirthing, also called the Mongan Method. These childbirth education classes are enhanced with self-hypnosis techniques. The classes emphasize the natural instincts of a woman for a more comfortable birthing experience.

Your health care provider probably knows where these classes are being given or you can check the internet for teachers and classes in your neighborhood.

Cesarean

In some cases your doctor will recommend a Cesarean (C-Section) when a vaginal birth is not possible or safe for you or your baby. Difficulties can include breech position where the baby is poised to come out buttocks or feet first, premature labor with complications, multiple babies or placenta previa, which means that the placenta is lying unusually low in your uterus. Your C-Section can be scheduled in advance

Here are a few ideas that may be helpful during labor:

- Have someone give you massages, especially on your lower back and feet.

- Bring things that keep your mind occupied such as books, magazines, and music.

- Create an environment that you like by dimming the lights, playing your favorite music, limiting the amount of people in your room, or all of the above.

- Take a warm bath or shower.

- Move as much as you want and can. Let your partner help you walk the hallway, hang on him, dance.

- Remember the tips from the childbirth classes. Use breathing techniques.

- Try different positions. Use the bed, sofa or sink to hold on. Try to stand on hands and knees, move around.

but sometimes it is necessary to perform the surgery, should complications arise, during labor such as when the baby can not fit through the birth canal or there is marked fetal distress.

At a planned C-Section you will get a regional anesthetic (spinal) that numbs the lower half or your body while enabling you to still be awake and alert. Once the anesthesia has taken effect, your doctor makes an incision through all the layers in your abdomen and uterus. The water inside the uterus will be suctioned out and the doctor gently lifts out the baby. The umbilical cord is cut and the baby's breathing is checked on right away. After the placenta is removed, the uterus and abdomen are closed with sutures and the skin is closed with sutures or staples.

Recovery from a C-Section is often longer and more uncomfortable than recovery from a vaginal birth. You aren't allowed to lift anything heavier than your newborn until your incision heals, usually within 6 weeks. So, you can't lift your other children and will probably need more help for the first two weeks, possibly longer.

Observations after the Delivery

A newborn baby will be checked right after it is born.

Apgar-score

One minute after birth the doctor will determine the Apgar score of your baby. This first impression score assesses the baby's heartbeat, breathing, muscle tone, response capacity, and skin color and allows the doctor to judge how well your baby is doing physically. For each category the baby can get 0, 1 or 2 points. After 5 minutes, and sometimes again at 10, the same check is performed again. At the second or third check the baby usually scores higher. Most babies score between 7 and 10 points. As brand new parents you probably won't notice these checks.

Appearance of the Baby

Your baby, who will most likely be put on your belly right after delivery, will look wet and greasy. A white greasy substance is still on his skin. This greasy substance called vernix protects the baby's skin from the amniotic fluid in which it spends nine months floating. The vernix can make your baby smell sweet.

Some feel it is good to let this remain on the baby's skin for the first 24 hours because it still protects the skin while others prefer to wipe it off and give the baby a bath in the 1st hour after delivery.

Because the baby has been in an oxygen-poor environment the skin color looks bluish-gray right after delivery. As soon as the baby cries, however, the skin will gradually turn to a normal pink color. The skin can be blotchy the first days of life. Babies with a darker skin tone often have blue/gray spots on their skin. These are called 'Mongolian spots.' After a few weeks these will go away on their own or fade. Spots on the back and shoulders usually take a lot longer to disappear.

The head can take on an unusual shape due to the trauma of delivery and your baby's genitalia and breasts often emerge red and swollen. This is nothing to worry about. Within a few days, these issues will resolve naturally.

Reflexes

Every baby has certain reflexes from birth that enable him to survive. Reflexes are checked to ensure your baby is neurologically healthy. Here is a description of a few of these reflexes.

If you rub against your baby's cheek, his head will turn in the direction of your breast and his mouth will instinctively search for the nipple. As soon as he has it in his mouth, he will begin sucking and swallow the milk. This is called the rooting reflex.

The grasp reflex is easy noticeable if you touch the palm of your baby's hand. It will instantly grab your finger.

The baby also makes walking movements right after birth. If his foot touches the ground he will lift his leg and it looks like the baby 'steps up'. Besides these walking and placing reflexes, the baby also has a Startle and Moro reflex. With the Startle reflex, the baby reacts with his whole body if there is a sudden loud sound. The Moro reflex involves the movement of arms and legs into the air as if he is trying to hold on to something.

Vitamin K

Vitamin K helps blood clot and every newborn baby will get an injection of Vitamin K.

Antibiotic Eye Ointment

In most cases the newborn is also given some antibiotic eye drops or ointment. This is to prevent infections that can lead to blindness. These infections are caused by the same bacteria that cause gonorrhea or chlamydia in women and can be present in the vagina. As the baby travels through the birth canal, he could pick up those bacteria.

Crying

Birth is a very emotional event for you as well as for your baby. It is quite possible that your baby has to get used to his new environment. If your baby cries, then this is usually a sign that he's hungry. Always try to read your baby to see what is going on and why he is crying. You can comfort him by holding him close to you. Your smell, heartbeat and voice will give him a trusted feeling. A lot of babies are very tired after the birth, in which case, the baby will sleep a lot.

> After a while, you'll be able to recognize the meaning of each different cry:
> - The "I feel lonely" cry can be whiny
> - The "I have pain" cry can have long cries with long pauses
> - The "I am hungry" cry mostly sounds inpatient.

Observing the Baby

Now that the baby has left the uterus, his lungs, kidneys, liver, intestines and other organs have to function on their own. The lungs have to take in oxygen and remove carbon dioxide. The baby's blood changes. The liver needs to process these changes. The stomach and intestines have a task in taking in and digesting food. And the baby has to regulate its own temperature.

The nurse keeps a close eye on all of these changes. She looks at certain signals like the breathing rate and color of the baby that indicate the functioning of the lungs. Bowel movements and urination indicate the functioning of the kidney and intestines. The first bowel movement from a baby is black and tough. This is called meconium. The umbilical cord stub is also checked to make sure bleeding has stopped.

Baby's Airway and Breathing

If the baby swallows incorrectly, he can have trouble breathing. Keep your baby upright and tap it on the back. If this doesn't resolve the problem right away, call the nurse immediately. If it does resolve, be sure to inform the nurse about the event after it occurs. Make sure that baby's clothes fit loosely around the neck and chin, so that any fluid can come out of his mouth. Wrapping gauze around your finger, like a thimble, can help remove oral secretions. The baby will cry and spit the mucous out. Ask a nurse to show you how to do this.

Checking the Mother after Delivery

Uterus

The uterus will contract after delivery. The blood vessels that were connected to the placenta have to close. A well-contracted uterus will feel hard and firm. For the first few hours after delivery, regular checks by your nurse will monitor the condition of your uterus, if you have any discharge, and your recovery from the delivery. Massaging the uterus is important for the first 24 hours to help the uterus contract. The nurse will instruct you on this. During the first days

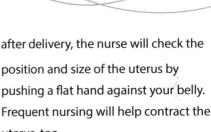

after delivery, the nurse will check the position and size of the uterus by pushing a flat hand against your belly. Frequent nursing will help contract the uterus, too.

Going to the Restroom

The emptier the bladder, the easier it is for the uterus to contract. It is important to use the restroom as soon as you can after delivering your baby once it is safe to do so. Your hospital-issued collection of goodies will probably include a plastic squeeze bottle that you can fill with lukewarm water to spray on your vagina should it hurt to pee. This may also be the best method for clean-up if you are contending with episiotomy stitches as well. Try to urinate every two to three hours to avoid a distressed bladder. Your baby is not pushing on your bladder anymore to remind you to go frequently.

If you are planning on breastfeeding your baby, then make sure you start within 1 hour after birth. If you are planning on bottle-feeding, discuss with the nurse when would be the best time to start.

The First Feeding

Every child is different. Sometimes babies long for the breast right after they are born while others need to be inspired by offering them the breast.

To stimulate breastfeeding, the baby is presented the breast as soon as possible, preferably within an hour after delivery. The nurse, midwife, or doula can help you with this. It is also very good to give the baby a chance to nurse at least eight times a day or even more for the first two days. Lie down on your side and find a comfortable position for yourself. Your baby should turn his head toward your nipple if you touch his cheek. He will open his mouth in search of milk. Let the baby take the whole nipple in the mouth, including the areola

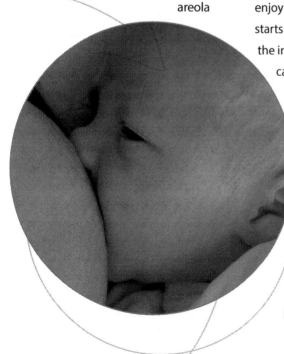

(dark part). The colostrum, the very first mother's milk, looks transparent and creamy and contains important antibodies for the baby. You could say the colostrum is the baby's very first vaccination. After a few days you will see whiter mother's milk. For more information about breastfeeding check the separate chapter in this book.

The First Hours after Delivery

The New Mother

There's your baby. After nine long months the baby is finally in your arms and you can gaze upon his little face. The long waiting, the delivery, it's all over now that your baby is there. Hopefully everything is going well. Does your baby feel like it is yours right away or do you have to get used to being a mother?

At first most parents are happy and relieved that everything was successful and that their child is healthy. It's time to enjoy the new baby. But with that also starts a time of changing moods. After the initial swell of relief, other feelings can start rearing their heads.

To start, physically your body is not quite as it was nine months ago. While your body is healing from the delivery, your breasts are starting to produce milk, even if you are not planning on breastfeeding.

Your breasts will feel big and solid. Your lower region may have sutures that are not yet healed. As tired as you may be,

your excitement may keep you from sleeping. And if you do nod off, you will wake up often because a hungry baby is crying for you.

Just like you have to get used to your pregnancy, you have to get used to this new situation. You have become a mother. The responsibility you feel for this little child that depends on you can weigh awfully heavy on you. Despite the fact that most of the time you probably feel happy, you may be welling up with tears regularly. The people that care for you in this special period of time know that these mixed feelings are there. Every new mother has them. Don't be too hard on yourself. It is important that you take time with your loved ones during these special moments.

Of course every woman is different, but physically you can expect the following things to happen in the next few days:

- You may perspire a lot more, especially at night.

- Bowel movements will start slowly and fret not if you're a bit scared to push, especially if you have sutures.

- During breastfeeding you might feel unpleasant cramp-like contractions in your uterus. This means your uterus is getting smaller.

- The first few days, you lose a lot more blood than during a normal period. But it should progressively lessen and will change into yellow/white discharge.

The Newborn Baby

In the uterus, the baby gets everything he needs through the umbilical cord. From the moment the baby is born, he will have to do everything on his own. The heart pumps blood to the lungs that open when the baby takes his first breath. The baby will start drinking, as well as urinating and stooling.

On the top of the head of every newborn are two soft spots called the fontanels. These are openings between the two parts of the skull. Thanks to the fontanels, the baby was afforded an easier passage through the birth canal. After the fist year, these fontanels will close on their own.

Even if your baby feeds well, it is normal for him to lose weight the first few days. The weight loss should not be more than 10 percent of the baby's original weight. If so, contact your doctor. Very small and very large babies may require extra monitoring.

Newborn babies have an irregular breathing pattern and sometimes make noises when they breathe in and out. This is very normal. The little nose doesn't have nose hairs yet which explains why they can suddenly sneeze, and by sneezing the baby can keep its airway clear. The sense of smell of a newborn is very well developed. Many babies move a lot, these are reflexive movements. They don't yet have control over their movements.

Don't smoke near the baby. It is very bad for their young lungs.

A newborn needs love, affection, and safety. If your baby keeps on crying, it is always best to pick him up and comfort him.

Babies love cuddling and attention. The more contact you have with your baby, the easier it will be to understand your baby and you can satisfy his needs. In the first half year of their life, it is not possible to spoil a baby. Comfort and cuddle your baby as much as you can. He will learn that he won't be abandoned if he needs affection.

It is absolutely not necessary to let a baby cry in order to strengthen its lungs. They will get strong by themselves.

Delivery Report

The delivery report is a place to document everything that happened during delivery and the first few hours after that. The hospital probably uses their own report that can be used by colleagues like the pediatrician, doctor, nurse, doula and midwife to inform each other about the delivery and the condition of you and your baby. You can find the delivery report in the back of this book. Keep it with you whenever you visit a doctor or midwife in the first few weeks after delivery.

For the First Time Together

After your delivery, in the hospital or at home, and once everything has been checked, cleaned and taken care of, you will be alone with your baby for the first time. It may feel a bit unreal, and you will probably be tired. Please rely on the people around you to help you during these first days. Try to enjoy the moment and ask all the questions you have about how to best take care of your baby and your own body.

In the Hospital

If you delivered your baby in the hospital, you will probably be taken care of in a special maternity ward amongst other newborns and mothers. Some rooms are private, others are shared. The nursing staff is specially trained and well aware of the new situation you are in. Do not hesitate to ask any question about ways to care for your baby. They have lots of experience and can give you a lot of advice.

Most insurance companies will allow you to stay in the hospital for 2 nights after a vaginal delivery. If you had a Cesarean, a few more days will be included. A Cesarean is a major surgery and your wound should be healed enough before you go home. The doctor will decide when you and your baby will be discharged from the hospital.

At Home

Regardless of whether or not you delivered at home or have just returned home from the hospital, you will need extra help. Ask a family member or friend. Or, if you can, hire a nurse or doula to help you during the first few days. She both helps with and advises you on the care of the baby. You can ask every question there is and she will give you useful tips about bathing, feeding schedules, sleeping schedules, etc. She will help you through those first exciting days, so that you can resume your 'normal' life again with the confidence that you can take good care of your baby on your own.

This book is especially made for those first days after the delivery of your baby. Use it as much as you can. It can answer a lot of questions that you can't always directly ask someone else.

The Partner

For the partner the arrival of a baby can mean big changes too. The new mother and baby get all the attention and care. Partners might think to themselves; "Is there any role for me in this?" Certainly. What goes for the mother also goes for the partner. Make yourself comfortable with this little new life by hugging, snuggling and gazing at it. Help with your baby's care and you will start to develop a bond together. Remember to not only take care of the mother and baby, but also yourself.

The New Mother

The Ob-Gyn/ Midwife and Pediatrician

During the first few days the Ob-gyn/ midwife and pediatrician will regularly

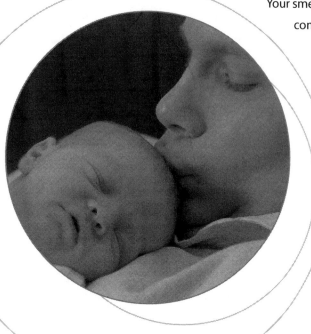

check on you and the baby to ensure that recovery is going well. Additional appointments will be scheduled ranging from later in the week to later in the month.

Vaginal Bleeding

It is important that you don't lose too much blood. Don't panic if you are enduring a heavy blood flow. However you should contact you doctor immediately if you are using more then two big pads an hour, because you are probably losing too much blood.

The Newborn

Belly Button Stump

The remaining stump of the umbilical cord will change from yellowish green to brown to black as it shrivels and falls off, usually within the first 2 weeks. It is not abnormal for the stump to smell.

Crying

Birth is also a very traumatic event for the baby. The baby needs to get to know his new surroundings. If the baby cries, keep him close to comfort him. Your smell, heartbeat and voice can be comforting. A lot of babies are tired from being born. In that case, let the baby sleep. But make sure you don't let your baby sleep for more than 4 hours at a time, because it keeps your baby from being fed at such an important stage of its life.

Feeding

The nurse will discuss with you when and how

you can best feed your baby. Make notes if you don't want to forget. For more information on breastfeeding and bottlefeeding, check the separate chapter in this book.

Positioning your Baby in Bed

Baby's safest position in bed is on the back. Do not lay your baby down on the belly to go to sleep.

Never lay your baby down on a waterbed. The motion can roll the baby over onto his tummy increasing the risk of suffocation.

Circumcision

When you have a boy, you have an important decision to make, whether or not to circumcise him. In a circumcision, the foreskin is surgically removed, exposing the end of the penis. This procedure is generally done within 2 days after birth. Some religious faiths perform ritual circumcisions after discharge from the hospital.

The reason to opt for a circumcision is often based on religious beliefs and hygienic concerns as well as cultural or social reasons (perhaps the family wants their son to look like the other men in the family). It is not a medically necessary procedure.

The decision to have your son circumcised is yours. You may want to think and talk about it before your due date. Check out the pros and cons of the procedure and discuss them with your doctor or pediatrician, who will most likely perform the procedure.

Caring for a Circumcised Penis

Gently clean the area with water every day as well as at every diaper change.

Most doctors prefer to protect the area with a gauze pad and ointment. You might need to apply a new one whenever you change his diaper for the first week. Put petroleum jelly on the gauze pad so it won't stick on his skin. A dab of petroleum jelly on the baby's penis will prevent any potential discomfort he may experience from rubbing against the diaper. It usually takes between 7 to 10 days for the penis to heal.

Call your doctor if:

- The wound doesn't stop bleeding

- Your son doesn't have a wet diaper within 6 to 8 hours after the circumcision

- The redness and swelling around the tip of the penis do not go away after 3 to 5 days

- There is a yellow discharge around the tip of the penis after 7 days

- Your son has a fever of 100.4 F or higher

For more information about circumcisions, check the internet or ask your pediatrician.

_____ **was born on**_____ **at**_____**hour.**

Our first moments as new parents :

Our babies first picture:

Whether you are at home or in the hospital on day 2, try to get as much rest as you can. You probably have some extra help around. Take advantage of all the help you can get. Gather as much information as you need about taking care of your baby. Let someone show you how to bathe your baby, change a diaper and help you with feeding (breast or bottle).

Checks on the Baby

In the days after the delivery, the nurse or pediatrician will check on your baby. This way, any problems adjusting to the life outside the uterus can be detected early.

Explanations of what is being checked by the pediatrician

Breathing

The respiratory system might be a bit immature at birth. Because of this, the baby's breathing may be slightly irregular during the first few months. Call your doctor or 911 right away if you ever see the baby in distress or breathing consistently fast as this is an emergency.

Body Temperature

A newborn baby isn't very good at maintaining its own temperature. A standard temperature ranges between 98º F (36.5ºC) and 100.4 ºF (38º C). Cold baby hands are normal, but it is important that the neck of the baby feels the same temperature as your hand. If the temperature is higher or lower than normal, please check with the doctor immediately.

Weight

Most babies weigh between 3200 and 3800 grams (7lbs and 8.4 lbs) when they are born. In the first few days, a newborn baby could lose up to 10% of its bodyweight.

Color of the Baby

Keep an eye on your baby's skin tone as it's the best way to monitor its oxygen supply. With optimal circulation the skin is a nice pink. If the skin looks 'yellow' this could be because the liver isn't yet functioning optimally and can't get rid of all of the bilirubin in the bloodstream. This causes the jaundice (yellow color) and would usually develop 2 or 3 days after birth.

This is normal and generally resolves naturally in the first few weeks because of increased feedings and active digestion. It is helpful to nurse the baby in indirect

---

Your pediatrician will monitor the following aspects and you may want to as well:

- Feeding, urinating, stooling, and sweating

- Body temperature

- The color of the baby when active or excited

- Breathing: do you already recognize a breathing rhythm?

- Sleeping rhythm: how and when does your baby sleep and for how long?

- Hunger signals

sunlight. The pediatrician should see your baby if jaundice develops. She may want to have the baby's blood level checked for bilirubin. Sometimes, babies need special light therapy to help resolve the jaundice quickly.

Feeding

Discuss with your nurse or doctor when and how you are going to feed your baby. A feeding schedule can be established which is very helpful in the first few days. There are people whose area of expertise revolves solely around everything concerning breastfeeding. They are called lactation specialists and can be found in hospitals, doctors'/mid-wifes offices, or on their own.

You can find all the information about breast and bottle feeding in the special section of this book.

Spitting-up

It is normal when a baby spits-up. Sometimes he isn't able to swallow the last drops of milk because he is already full.

He could be feeding too fast or not getting 'burped' often enough. If he is vomiting with a decrease in wet diapers or if he seems in pain after feeding, then notify the pediatrician.

Bowel Movement

Your baby's bowel movements will become lighter and lighter after the first black, tar-like meconium. Normal breastfeeding stools are yellow and seedy. Your newborn should make at least one bowel movement a day but could have as many as eight to ten a day. It varies from baby to baby.

Peeing

For the first few days, the baby will go through a minimum of two or three wet diapers a day. After that, there should be a wet diaper before or after almost every feeding. If your baby has no wet diaper for 12 hours after a normal pattern is established, call the pediatrician.

Should you discover an orange colored discharge in the diaper within the first few days or weeks, it will most likely be crystallized urine salts but you should bring your baby and the diaper to the pediatrician to be evaluated. This could indicate dehydration.

Girls could have a little bit of discharge (blood/slime) in the diaper because of hormonal changes. This will go away by itself and isn't harmful.

Skin

Some babies have pearly white bumps on their face and sometimes body, or a red

Some blood is drawn from the baby's heel within 48 hours. The blood will be tested for some rare but serious diseases such as PKU (phenylketonuria), thyroid abnormalities and sickle cell anemia.

The baby's hearing will also be tested. This is a painless test to detect hearing deficits at an early stage.

splotchy rash on their cheeks or body. How attractive! The red rash is called erythema toxicum and seems to be the result of the skin adjusting to life outside the uterus. The white bumps across your baby's nose and chin are called milia. Both complexion problems are not pretty, but they're common and temporary. They will disappear on their own after a few weeks. In the meantime, wash your baby's face with warm water two or three times a day and pat it dry. Don't use lotions, oils or other treatments. Never pinch or scrub milia or the red rash.

Dry and scaly skin will resolve after one to two weeks. You don't need to use lotion or creams. Enlarged breasts can be seen because of mom's hormones. These also will eventually disappear without incident.

Monitoring you as a New Mother

Not only is your baby being checked regularly in the first few days following delivery, so are you. Delivery is a tremendous effort, emotionally as well as physically and so your recovery should be monitored carefully.

Explanation of the Checks

Breast

Regardless of what type of feeding you offer your baby, your breasts will be swollen. Check your breasts daily for irregularities.

Discharge

The placenta wound will be healing during the next few weeks. This will cause vaginal bleeding and discharge. The discharge can occur for several weeks. If you are very active it can flow stronger. If the discharge smells unpleasant there could be an infection, check with your

doctor. Do not use tampons.

Perineum

The perineum is the area between the anus and vagina. After giving birth naturally this will feel tender and swollen. Because of the wound and, for many women, possible sutures, the perineum is very susceptible to infections. Stay off your feet as much as possible and try to do some Kegel exercises to increase blood flow to the area which will encourage healing. You can find Kegel exercises in the separate exercise chapter of this book.

Urine and Bowel Movements

During your pregnancy your body holds about two to three liters of extra fluid. After delivery this extra fluid will leave your body. You will notice this because you may perspire more and go to the bathroom more often than usual. For some women, it can take about three days before your intestines will work well enough again to allow you to have a bowel movement. The loss of fluid and minimal activity during your first days after delivery may make your first stool's consistency fairly hard, hence another good reason to drink a lot of water right now. At least 2 liters a day. You could also consider using stool softener.

For some women it is difficult, not to mention a little bit scary, to strain to pass stool. Still it is very important that your bowels start working again. To help your body with this, try to drink a glass of lukewarm water on an empty stomach, eat whole grains and green vegetables. This will work as a stool softener.

Talking

It is a good thing to talk with someone about how you are feeling and how your day went. It doesn't matter if it is to your partner, nurse, or someone else who helps you. Let them know how you feel and what you need. Also discuss things like the number of visitors you want, rest times, the other kids-schedules, meals, etc. Things can be changed as long as you let others know what works for you.

Birth certificate and social security number

The hospital staff or your midwife will give you the first documentation on the birth of your child. They will provide you with the forms that will enable you to obtain a certified copy of the original birth certificate. The same forms will allow you to apply for a social security number on behalf of your child. You'll receive the birth certificate and social security card by mail. The internet can provide you with a lot of information about both. Check out www.ssa.gov/people/kids and click on 'numbers for children' for help.

You will probably get a lot of other paperwork, footprints of your baby, general healthcare information, telephone numbers, etc. The back of this book offers the perfect place to save them all together.

Practical Notes from Day to Day

In this chart you can make notes every day about your feeding schedule and your baby's output.

Time

In the 'time' section you can note the feeding times.

Type of feeding

Breastfeeding notes should include which side (a.k.a. which breast) you used and for how long, perhaps you switched sides mid-feed. Did you pump and then bottle feed? Did you use formula? How much did the baby drink?

Spitting up

If and how much did the baby spit up.

Urine and bowel movement

What was in the diaper and how many diapers were there? This is to see if your baby is hydrated enough.

Remarks

Anything you would like to add that you don't want to forget.

If you write down all of your observations every day, you can compare them with the previous days, giving you insight into your baby's habits and rhythms. This is a valuable information source for your pediatrician, too. Take it with you to your baby's first appointment.

Daily Observations Day 2 (example)

Time	Type of Feeding	Spitting Up	Urine	Bowel Movement	Remarks
7am	Breast (both, stopped left)		yes		Baby really hungry
10am	Breast (both, stopped left)	little	yes		
1pm	Breast (one, right)		yes		pumped some milk
4pm	Breast (left and right, stopped right)		yes		
7:30pm	Breast (started right, stopped left	little	yes	yes	
11pm	Pumped breastmilk with bottle	little	yes	yes	My husband tried while I slept
1:30am	Breast (both, stopped left		yes		
4am	Breast (both, stopped right				

A daily observation chart for the first 14 days is added in the back of this book.

Our first night together was :

Our baby looks like:

Room for pictures :

day 3

This is the day you will go home with your newborn if you delivered your baby in the hospital and didn't have a Cesarean or complications. You will take your little wonder in a safe baby carrier for his first ride home. There you are, all alone with this tiny little human being. Scared, emotional, happy, concerned... everything comes together. And your own body is changing tremendously, too. Hopefully you will have some extra help for a few days when you get home. This could be your partner, a doula or nurse, a relative, friend or neighbor. You can use this book to help with a lot of the basic things that you will need to do and answer questions that will come up. If you have any concerns or are not sure, please contact a professional like your doctor. Most importantly, enjoy your newborn baby. This sounds like a cliché, but they do grow so fast. Take the time to appreciate each nuance of these precious first weeks.

What Now?

You have to learn how to take care of your baby. Hopefully you have had someone sharing a lot of information with you in the hospital and at home already. You have already been shown basic skills, like how to change a diaper and bathe your baby. You can also check out the special chapters about these things in this book.

About the Baby

Fontanels

At this young stage, you'll notice that your baby's skull has two soft spots where the bones of the skull meet. These fontanels allow the skull to compress during the journey through the birth canal but will fuse together in about one year. Always be aware to make sure that nothing hard hits the baby's head during the first few months. This could be very dangerous.

Crying

Every baby cries on average for about one to two hours a day for different reasons. Crying is the only way for the baby to let you know that there is something going on. For the first few days, it might be difficult for you to understand your baby's different cries. But, given a little bit of time, if you listen carefully, you might discover that his cry is different when he is hungry, has a dirty diaper, feels lonely, or is uncomfortable.

If your baby cries with an abnormally high-pitch and this is something you haven't heard before, something could be wrong medically and you should contact the doctor.

Gas

Your baby can get uncomfortable because he has gas. A baby with gas will likely pull his legs up while he is crying. When you breastfeed you need to realize that the things that you eat will influence the composition of your milk. Some things you eat can give your baby gas. You will have to figure out by trial and error which foods cause this. Improper latching, where the baby gulps air instead of milk, can also be a gas culprit.

A few tips to relieve the gas:

- Burp your baby frequently.

- While feeding your baby, keep him more upright and rub his back.

- Put a warm cloth over the baby's stomach. Test the cloth on your own skin first to make sure it is not too hot for the baby.

- Give the baby a warm bath.

- Gently make bicycle movements with the baby's legs.

- Lay the baby with his belly on your arm (see picture below).

If you bottle-feed your baby, check with a nurse or other professional for additional helpful tips. Sometimes formula brands have a help line to call for advice.

About the New Mom

Tiredness

You have delivered an absolute top performance from which you now have to recover. Some young mothers feel so wonderful that they think they can do anything. But remember: while delivery is not an illness, it certainly asks a lot from your body. Fatigue will halt a speedy recovery. That's why it is essential that you get enough rest. Listen to your own body and don't let stories of others who tell you that they could do everything right after delivery rush you. Recovering from a delivery is not a game and you don't have to prove anything to anybody.

Everybody is different and will recover in their own way. Get enough rest in bed and you will feel better sooner. This is especially important during the night feedings stage. Try to rest in bed or on the couch for an hour or more during the day. Do get up on a regular schedule and try to find the right balance between rest and activity. It will make you a happier mom.

Breasts

Because of hormonal changes in your body, the milk glands are starting to produce milk. If you are not going to breastfeed your baby, then put on a firm, supporting bra to halt the milk production. To prevent your breasts from filling up with milk, keep your bra on during showering. And don't point the water directly on your breasts as it will stimulate the milk production.

Engorgement

A few days after the delivery, your breast may be swollen and incredibly tender due to engorgement. This develops because the body is sending more blood and fluids to your breasts. Moreover the milk production is increasing rapidly. You can reduce if not prevent engorgement by breastfeeding your baby often the first few days and nights. As soon as the milk production is readjusted to the needs of your baby, the engorgement will disappear. Often this takes a few days. If you carefully position the baby at your breast the normal 'let down' reflex will provide

milk for your baby. You can stimulate this reflex by putting warm compresses on your breasts before feeding. The warm compress can also reduce the pain. Take enough time for feeding.

If your breasts are really painful and engorged you can try to get some relief by;

- Putting a cold compress on your breasts after feeding (cold washcloth or cold crushed kale leaves). Don't do the kale if you have nipple cracks.

- Use different positions during feeding. The breast will be emptied just a little bit differently by doing that which will further relieve the pressure.

- If this isn't working, pump your breasts empty one time and if necessary repeat that again.

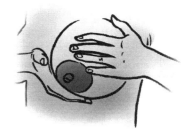

Sometimes the engorgement is so severe that your baby isn't able to 'latch on'. The best thing you can do is to pump your breast a little bit first, so that the nipple becomes a bit softer and the baby can try again. You can pump with a manual or electrical pump but also by hand. Check the special breastfeeding section in this book for more information.

Don't forget to fill in your daily observations for day 3 in the back.

Today we got a visit from:

The sweetest gifts :

Room for pictures :

Day 4 is probably one of the most emotional and, for most women, uncomfortable days. Nice to know, right?!? Everything comes together around this day. Your breasts will really start to swell and ache just as the bottom part of your body is also pulling and pushing. And your tears are ready to flow at moment's notice. Are the baby blues kicking in?

Watch your Baby

The baby needs to get adjusted to life outside your belly. The adjustment will usually take about 4 days. Watch your baby's growth and development with care. You can find more information about feeding and how you can tell if your baby feeds enough in the special breastfeeding chapter of this book.

Noting your observations in the charts for each day will allow you to compare these important things daily and recognize your baby's habits.

Growing

Most children weigh between 3200 and 3800 grams (7 and 8.3 pounds) when they are born. Girls often are a little bit lighter. Second children generally weigh a little bit more than the first. The first few days the baby will lose weight as he excretes more fluid than he takes in while feeding. Most babies don't receive more than 10 milliliters (1/3 oz) of milk a feeding these first days. This will slowly go up. After about 10 to 14 days, the baby should be back to his initial birth weight. After that, as everything has adjusted, he will continue to gain about one ounce per day until he is six months old.

Sutures

After a few days the sutures might pull or feel painful. There are a few ways to lessen the pain. First of all, flush your vagina with lukewarm water while you are urinating. Another way to do this is to urinate while you are in the shower. You can also place an ice pad (in a washcloth) against your vagina – try freezing a soaked sanitary pad and wrap it in a sealed bag. Once it is frozen you can use it, but don't forget to wrap it in a washcloth or some kind of house linen as to avoid freezing your skin. Ouch.

The Ob-Gyn
Unless you encounter complications or concerns, the six-week mark is where you will probably find yourself visiting your Ob-Gyn/midwife for a follow-up to ensure that you are recovering well.

With good hygiene you can prevent infections. Therefore it is of great importance to wash your hands before and

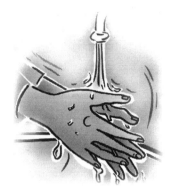

after you visit the restroom. Also, keep the area around your perineum clean by washing it carefully with water and flushing with water after each restroom visit. Change your pads regularly. Wearing slippers from the moment you step out of bed will reduce the chance of infections.

Emotions

Giving birth to a baby is very intense, especially when it is your first child. You will need to relieve all the tension whether you realize it exists or not. Changes in your hormones make you feel out of balance emotionally. The so-called 'baby blues' tears tend to make their presence known on the third or fourth day after delivery. It will probably coincide with the one wretched day when your engorged breasts ache like nothing you've ever felt. To the relief of many, but not all, these tears will often be over after a day or two.

Fill in your daily observations for day 4.

We named our baby_____   **because** _____

_____

_____

_____

_____

_____

_____

day 5

Your breasts are still achy and you're probably starting to feel now that sleep is a luxury. Are you staring at your baby all the time? Have you ever seen such a beautiful sight? The first week is all about starting up, adjusting to the situation and your baby, as well as the healing of your own body. Try to enjoy the special moments and cheer up, you are a mom now!

Sleeping

A baby who is a few weeks old sleeps about fifteen hours of the daily 24 hours. But there are no rules about how much sleep your baby needs. While this varies for every baby, remember that newborns need a lot of rest. Take that into consideration when you are expecting visitors.

Sleeping and Eating

You don't have to wake up the baby if it falls asleep during daytime feedings. Your baby will take more at the next feed. Some babies will begin to skip some nighttime feedings when they are six to eight weeks old. In the first month of life, babies should not go more than 4 hours without a feed. They need around the clock feeds for proper brain development.

Ears

It is okay to clean the outside of the ears and the skin around it. You can do this with a damp washcloth or a ball of cotton. Never use a cotton swab inside the baby's ear.

Eyes

You can clean your baby's eyes with a damp cotton ball and fresh water. Always move from the outside inward towards the nose. For every sweep use a new, clean cotton ball.

Eye Color

Shortly after birth almost all Caucasian babies will have pale skin and bluish colored eyes. Within a few weeks the eyes could turn brown or grey. It can take up to a year for the eyes to turn their definite color. Children with more exotic ethnic backgrounds tend to have brown eyes from the beginning.

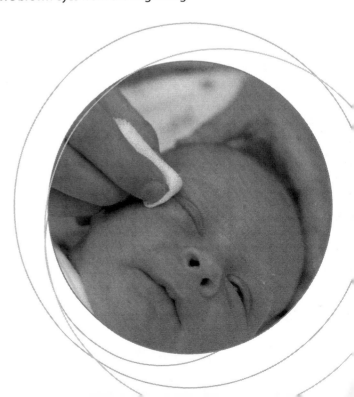

Lowering of the boys' testicles

Towards the end of the pregnancy, your baby boy's testicles will lower into the scrotum. Right after birth the doctor will confirm that this has happened. Sometimes the lowering will happen shortly after birth. If you bathe your baby, you can see if the testicles are lowered. When the baby is cold or gets scared the testicles can retract back into the stomach area. They return to the lower position when the baby is warm and comfortable. Your pediatrician will check to ensure that the testicles are present. You can also check it yourself by gently palpating the scrotum. Each testicle feels like a very small almond. You should feel two.

Think about your "Day 5" observations and write them down.

Diaper Check

You can see from the amount of urine the baby produces how much fluid it receives. Check your baby regularly for a wet diaper. If the diaper continues to be dry for 5 to 6 hours, contact your doctor.

Your birth announcement:

This is what my grandmas have to say about me:

day 6

How are you doing? How is feeding the baby going? If you are breastfeeding, don't expect it to go smooth already. Both you and your baby are just starting to learn. You can't ride a bike the first time your feet touch the pedals and the same goes for breastfeeding. It takes practice and time.

And is the father changing diapers? You can find all the information about breastfeeding, bathing your baby, and changing a diaper in the separate special chapters accompanied by a lot of pictures to make it easy for everyone to follow.

Thrush

Thrush is an often seen oral fungal infection characterized by white patches in the baby's mouth that can't be wiped away. There are a few extra hygienic steps you can try to get rid of it. Use a gauze pad to clean any milk residue from the baby's mouth and give him a little sip of cooled boiled water. Breastfeeding moms can also get hit with this infection. Sometimes you can be bothered by the infection even before you see the spots in the baby's mouth. Your nipples are irritated and your breasts feel painful, although they look normal. Clean your breasts with a soft cloth after each feeding. Thrush can also cause nipple cracks. Always consult your doctor when one of you develops thrush. You and your baby can be prescribed medication to treat the infection and to prevent infecting each other.

Boil materials like breast pump accessories (those that come into contact with your skin) and bottles for at least 10 minutes to sterilize them and always wash your hands. Replace pacifiers every week.

Other Children

It is a natural response for the mother to be primarily occupied with the newborn, but it is also very important to give the other children in the family some attention. Their entire home situation has changed. Everybody needs to find their new place in the family. If this doesn't go very well, try to ask someone to help out in the house so you can have more time dealing with this.

Older children often like to be involved in taking care of the baby. They can help bathing the baby. They can help fetch things for you. As long as they feel as if they have a positive purpose and impact in regards to the little one, things should go well.

Check your daily observations charts.

Our day today was:

I feel like:

Breastfeeding is:

Exercise

Once you finally feel that you are a little rested again, you can start with some light exercises. We are talking about exercises at home in bed, not in the gym! It is wise to discuss any kind of exercise with your doctor first. And this is only for woman who had a vaginal delivery, if you had a Cesarean you should wait a lot longer. See the information about a C-section (on page 47).

You will feel better faster if you start with some easy exercises a week after delivery. But do start easy and the exercises should not be painful. It is best to work in (very) short sessions a few times a day. Don't forget to breathe well and preferably from the stomach or diaphragm. To practice this, put your hands on your belly and breathe in, in a way that your belly moves up into your hands. Your belly will pull in a little as you breathe out.

Pelvic Muscle Exercises or Kegel Exercises

Start with these as soon as you can! Lie down on your back with your knees bent and feet a little wide on the ground or a mattress. Try, while breathing out, to pull your anus in. Pull your pelvis forward a little and tighten the belly. Release everything again in reverse order. Relax for a few minutes. If this feels all right you can do this more often every day, even while you are sitting and feeding your baby. You can increase the intensity by tightening the belly a little longer (5 or 10 counts) but remember to breathe.

Abdominal Exercises

These are exercises (again only for woman who had a vaginal delivery) you can do in the postpartum period. Discuss them with your doctor first, however, before you start.

- Pull in your belly (abdomen) while breathing out, relax your belly while breathing in.

- Tilt your pelvis while you breathe out (the lower part of your back pushes into the mattress) and let loose as you breathe in.

- Lie down on your back with knees bent and feet flat on the ground or mattress. Tilt your pelvis to the back. Bring your knee to your chest while breathing out and put it back. Pull up the other knee and put back.

- Lie on your back with bent knees and feet flat on the ground or mattress. Put your hands crosswise on your belly to support your abdominals. Lift your head and shoulders while breathing out. Come back down to the ground while breathing in.

Stand on hands and knees:

- Pull in your abdominal and bottom muscles. Your back will be round.

- Turn your hips left and right, like you are dancing the samba

- Pull in your abdominal and bottom muscles and stretch one arm in front of you

- Pull in your abdominal and bottom muscles and stretch together with one arm crossed over your leg. Start with your right arm and left leg then switch.

Room for pictures :

You should be getting a lot more comfortable with your newborn now. And your own body is probably feeling a lot better after a week of healing and adjusting to the new situation. If you feel like it, you could take a walk outside with your baby or go for a short trip to the store. Stepping outside of your little cocoon will make you feel as if you're part of the world once again.

Growth Spurt

Normally, your breasts will produce enough milk for your baby. And a baby that grows needs more and more milk. Your breasts will increase milk production during a growth spurt. This is the time when the baby is hungrier than usual. Generally, if you give your baby milk more often, after a few days your breasts and your baby are used to the extra amount of milk and the new rhythm, although some women will generate even more than necessary and others, not so much. The growth spurt days will occur around the second week, after six weeks and, again, somewhere around three months and six months.

Sleeping Safely

The Bedroom

The best place for a baby to sleep is in a bedroom with a temperature of about 64° F (18°C). Keep an eye on how the sun shines into the room as this could cause higher temperatures during part of the day and the baby could get too hot.

The Bed

A good baby bed has:

- A firm layer on top of the mattress.

- No head cushions or pillows in the bed as these restrict the airflow around the baby and the baby could suffocate.

- There should be no loose toys that can strangle the baby. Do NOT install loose or fluffy bumper pads! Many pediatricians recommend avoiding bumpers altogether.

If you do use blankets, opt for light cotton blankets. These are the best for the baby, certainly during the first 2 years. Depending on the season, give your baby one or two blankets. Make the bed 'short' in a way that the feet of the baby almost touch the back of the baby bed. A short made bed will give the baby a feeling of security.

A preferred option is to use a swaddling blanket, which some research says results in better sleep for a longer amount of time as compared to not using a swaddling blanket. Or you can use a sleep sack pajama.

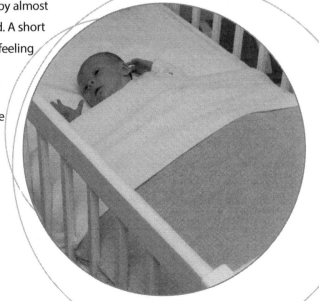

What is the safest sleeping method for your baby?

Always lay your baby down to sleep on his back. Never lay a baby on his belly. Although it remains unpredictable despite years of research, the first and foremost step to reduce the risk of sudden infants death syndrome (SIDS) is to put your baby to sleep on his back. A very recent study says that running a fan in a baby's room can also lower the risk of SIDS. By circulating air, fans may prevent infants

from breathing in exhaled carbon dioxide, a possible cause of SIDS.

Use cotton baby clothing for the baby as this offers the best ventilation.

Continue adding information to your daily observations chart 'Day 7' through 'Day 14.' Your pediatrician will be very happy to see your schedule and remarks.

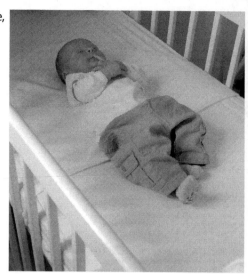

My life as a dad:

_____

_____

_____

_____

_____

_____

You typically:

_____

_____

_____

_____

_____

_____

Well-Checks at the Pediatrician

You've probably already scheduled your baby's well-check appointment with the pediatrician. At these well-check visits, the pediatrician looks at the baby's growth and development, recognizes problems early and reacts to them, and provides immunizations while advising you and answering all of your questions. Usually there will be a well-check 2 days after you come home from the hospital, at 2 weeks-old, again at 1 month and then monthly or every other month. Of course you must contact your health care provider any time your baby is ill or whenever you are concerned about the baby's health or development.

Special attention is paid to whether or not the baby has met the normal developmental milestones. Height, weight, and head circumference are recorded on a graph. For your own medical record of your baby you can write them down here.

How is your chart looking? Were you able to fill in something every day? Did you include a few remarks like a little diary? All this information could be very important for your next visit to the pediatrician. Try to complete as much as you can. In time, all of the things you are writing down now will later become precious memories upon which you'll enjoy reflecting. They also may be beneficial with your next baby, but let's not get ahead of ourselves.

Date visit pediatrician				
Age Baby				
Height				
Weight				
Head Circumference				

Room for pictures :

An Impression: A Day with Your Baby

The day mostly starts early for a baby. They say an adult doesn't know hunger only appetite. For a newborn this rule doesn't apply. They just are really very hungry. Your baby will let you know he's got this uncomfortable feeling by crying.

Feeding and Changing

Many mothers change their baby before feeding. There is a good reason for that: changing the diaper after feeding could add extra pressure to your baby's tummy. If your baby really cries after the feeding you can change the diaper then, too, but do it with gentle and easy movements.

If you are bottle-feeding, it is practical to have your bottle ready first, before you start changing.

Sit down comfortably, for example with a cushion or special feeding pillow under your arm where the baby can support his head. Make feeding a pleasant and relaxing time for yourself, too. If breastfeeding is still difficult, check out the special section in the back of this book for more tips. Read more about it or ask a doula or lactation specialist to help you. The need to suckle is very important for a newborn. Some babies like to nibble on your breasts for a long time but, for your breasts, this is not a very wise thing to do.

Growing

If you are breastfeeding you don't know exactly how much the baby is taking in but keeping an eye on the number of wet diapers is a good way to check if the baby is getting enough milk. There should be at least six every day. It can, by the way, take a few days before the diapers are starting to get really wet. You can also check the growth of your baby by weighing him.

Bathing

The morning is a good time to bathe your baby. A separate chapter of this book explains how to prepare this. Before you put the baby in the bath, you have to clean the eyes and buttocks of the baby. Be cautious with the use of soap as many skin problems are the result of using too much baby soap. Most babies are tired and want to sleep right after a bath. If you want to play and cuddle with your baby it is better to do that before and during the bath. And don't flip out, or even be surprised if baby pees or poops during the bathing process. Eventually he'll figure out that he doesn't want to do that.

The first weeks after delivery many babies need a feeding very regularly. Sometimes more than every two to three hours. After each feeding, place your baby with his head on your shoulder and softly tap on his back. Inspiring a burp to easily escape. This is even more important if you have a very fast drinker. If the air stays in the stomach the baby could become quite uncomfortable. Sometimes a baby will spit up some milk along with the burp. Put a cloth on your shoulder to keep your clothes clean.

Going Outside

During the day you can take your baby outside for a walk. If you are running errands, take your baby in a safe baby carrier or baby stroller. Don't let the sun shine directly on the baby's head. You can use a hat or umbrella for protection. If it is cold a hat is necessary too. Only use a rain cover on the stroller when it is raining. It gets very humid and warm under these covers. Avoid going to crowded places until the baby is at least 1 month old. Also avoid too many visitors in the first month and always

have them wash their hands or use hand sanitizer before touching the baby.

When your child nods off at home, take that time to rest or do some light work in the house. Or use that time to do something for yourself. Vacuuming while the baby sleeps is fine, because the steady noise of the machine isn't disturbing for the baby. Sometimes the noise of the vacuum is even used to calm the baby down to fall asleep. You will notice that your day will be scheduled around your child. His sleep schedule will end up determining what you can do and when. If you handle this in a relaxed fashion and don't stress yourself too much in what you 'must' do, you will adapt to the new rhythm fairly quickly.

You probably won't do much more with your baby the first few weeks than changing diapers, feeding, putting your baby down to sleep, and hugging. However, there are also 'active' babies that love to discover the world while being held close to you. Most babies do sleep several hours in a stretch.

If your baby doesn't feel good, the best thing to do is carry him on your arm. Your voice, touch, smell and attention give him comfort. You can also place the baby bed in your bedroom. A day with your baby doesn't end after the last feeding at around 11 p.m. The first few months, your baby needs a feeding or more in the middle of the night, too.

Healing: The End of the Pregnancy Body

After the first intense weeks, your body, which was totally dedicated to the pregnancy and pending delivery, will return back to its original function and form (more or less). Also your hormones will stabilize (if you are lucky). How long that will take and how that feels all depends on your general health before and during pregnancy, the type of delivery, and any complications during delivery and afterwards. For some women it doesn't take long to get totally back to a non-pregnancy body and state of mind. But for most women it takes a long time to be able to say, ' I am back to myself.' Sometimes a year or longer.

Usually, the initial recovery from a vaginal delivery is much more rapid than that of a C-section. Many women will feel better within a week or two of having a vaginal delivery, while women who have undergone C-section generally take more time to recuperate. Some general guidelines for activities after delivery are as follows:

Vaginal Delivery
After 1 week you can begin driving again and do some very light exercise on your bed. After 2 weeks you can add more light exercise such as walking and taking stairs.

At 6 weeks you will have your exam at the Ob-Gyn. If she is okay with it, you can resume most of your activities including an exercise regimen, sexual intercourse and work.

C-Section
After 2 weeks you have your post-operative check up. If everything is okay you can probably begin driving again. Before you get behind the wheel, you will need to have stopped taking narcotic pain medication and you should be comfortable slamming on the brakes of your car without thinking about whether or not your incision will hurt. Test yourself in the driveway before you pull out to make sure.

After 6 weeks you have your next exam at the Ob-Gyn. If she is ok with it, you can resume most of your activities including an exercise regimen, sexual intercourse and most other activities.

Getting Pregnant (again!)
Women can get pregnant while they breastfeed, even if they haven't yet had a menstrual period. If you don't want to get pregnant right away, then you need to discuss with your doctor what kind of contraception will work for you at this time.

If you breastfeed, you may very well go months without a period. When you bottle-feed your child, it will take about six weeks to have your first period again.

Besides the physical changes, you and your partner have to get used to a new family life. It will probably take a while before you have found your rhythm and everything is back to normal. Most women have a tough time the first few weeks taking care of themselves and the new baby, especially when the delivery wasn't easy. Uncertainties about parenthood come and go. Share your feelings with your partner. You aren't in it alone. You may be exhausted, at your wit's end, and feeling awfully yucky.

For that reason it is very important to take some time for yourself whenever you can. Take a nice warm bath, rest on the couch, revisit your make-up case 'cause you know you feel better when you look better.' Afford yourself this attention. Housekeeping can wait, you are more important right now! A happy mom is a better mom.

There are also women that don't have any problems adjusting to the new situation. The new baby blends into the family effortlessly and the big enjoyment can start right away. Why is it that such a life changing experience is difficult for one and easy for another? It depends on a lot of factors. That's why it is very hard to predict how you are going to react. Bottom line, never question yourself because it is all very natural.

Baby Blues

Every woman experiences the recovery from a delivery differently. Perhaps you'll recognize yourself in some of the following:

- Emotionally you don't feel very well and you don't know why. Your baby is doing great and is very sweet, you have a great partner, your house is organized, but you still don't feel completely happy. You imagined it differently.

- You have trouble sleeping.

- You don't feel fit, are tired, cry about anything and are very forgetful.

- You can't concentrate and focus as much as you used to.

This is called the 'baby blues' and usually begins the third day after birth, gets worse around the fifth day and then mostly ends about the tenth day after birth.

Postpartum Depression

If you feel that your baby blues are getting worse, noting one or more of the following symptoms, you need to contact your doctor right away!

- Great disturbance in your sleep patterns

- Depressed or sad mood

- Loss of appetite

- Low self-esteem

- Inability to care for yourself or your baby

  - Moderate to severe anxiety

  - Obsessive thoughts (thoughts that preoccupy you and won't go away)

  - Panic attacks (heart beats quickly, sweaty palms, sense of unreality, shortness of breath)

  - Thoughts of killing yourself or your baby

Support Networks

In the first year of being a new mom, support is crucial for you. The saying 'it takes a village to raise a child' is not just hot air. Right after birth you need help with the actual household chores and the care of other children. Later, having someone to talk to, ask advice from, or simply share your concerns and frustrations with, can make all the difference in the world. You might not realize it, but the perfect person with whom you can share your feelings might be right under your nose:

- Your own mother or mother-in-law

- Sisters and sisters-in-law

- Friends who are also new mothers

- New moms you know from childbirth educations classes

- Join a local parenting support group like the International Moms Club. Check the website www.momsclub.org or www.newcomersclub.com for parenting support groups in your area.

- See a therapist

Feeding Your Baby

What do you Choose?

During your pregnancy is it important to think about how you are going to feed your baby. Are you going to breastfeed or use formula? In general, breastfeeding is recommended for the health of your baby. But whatever you choose, it is your choice. Try to be informed about the pros and cons.

Here are some reasons why 'breast is best'

- Breast milk contains a lot of antibodies that can protect your baby against ear infections, airway infections, diarrhea and a host of other ailments.

- Breastfeeding reduces the risk of the baby developing allergies, eczema, childhood obesity and diabetes.

- Breast milk is always available and always the right temperature, wherever you are.

- By breastfeeding, your uterus contracts faster, there is a lesser chance of bleeding after delivery, and some say you will lose your pregnancy-weight faster.

- During breastfeeding you have intimate physical contact with your baby affording you both added security and comfort.

> If you deliver in the hospital make sure the nursing staff knows you intend to breastfeed!

- Breastfeeding is friendly to the environment and free.

- Scientific research has shown that by breastfeeding you lower the chance of getting some forms of cancer and bone decay.

- Breast milk is easier to digest and doesn't tax the baby's intestines as much as formula.

Breastfeeding is something you and your baby need to learn. You have to get used to each other and the way it works best. It's a little like riding a bike. During the first few weeks, you and your baby may struggle, and occasionally crash and burn. And then one day, you'll start peddling and ride for miles. It will be so easy you won't understand why you were ever having so much trouble. Your partner's help, support, encouragement, and assistance can be crucial in getting you started. Let him change diapers, comfort the baby, get the baby out of bed, etc. whenever possible.

Right After Delivery

The nicest thing to do right after delivery

> Depending on the weight of your baby, you should feed him on demand every 1½ to 3 hours with a minimum of 8-12 times per 24 hours.

is to hold your baby against your skin. If you do that, the baby will search for your breast within one hour. It is very important to latch the baby on within one hour. The baby is wide awake and the suckling reflex is very strong. If the baby is ready to go, he will let you know by searching for your nipple, licking, and moving the lips to grab your breast. Most babies sleep a lot the first few days. Do try to feed as often as possible. The breasts are still nice and soft the first few days which makes latching on easier for him. Your baby will have just enough mother's milk (colostrum) with the small sips it gets the first few days. After three to five days your milk production will start increasing and the baby will probably wants to feed every two to three hours. Before the baby starts to cry, he will show you that he's ready for another feeding by blinking his eyes, smacking his mouth or rooting around in search of food. Feeding on demand means giving the baby milk when he's hungry. Feed your baby at least eight times every 24 hours, and remember that many babies will feed 10-12 times a day. Most babies will establish a rhythm of demand within a few days.

The First Days

You need to learn how to breastfeed your baby. There are mothers and babies that have a natural talent for breastfeeding from day one. But in most cases it will take up to one or two weeks before you really can feel comfortable and enjoy breastfeeding. It simply takes a while for mother and baby to make a good team and find a good feeding rhythm. Nursing a well-latched baby doesn't hurt, but the first few days starting to nurse can be less than fun. If the nursing still is painful after the first 10 seconds then take the baby from your breast by putting your pinky in the corner of the baby's mouth and start all over again. The baby can breastfeed as long as he wants until he lets loose or doesn't suck firmly anymore.

After a small break, you can offer him the other breast until he is no longer sucking effectively. A feeding generally lasts about half an hour. The first milk that leaves the breast is called foremilk. Foremilk contains mainly water, milk sugars, and protective ingredients. The hindmilk that follows is much more fatty and energy rich. The baby needs both to grow well. If the baby gets enough by feeding only one side each time, that is okay, too, however don't forget to jot down which breast you used last. The more milk your baby takes, the more milk your milk glands will produce. Your breasts will never get completely empty, and milk production occurs around the clock, so very rarely does one have to worry about not producing enough milk.

Your Position During Nursing

You can nurse in different positions. It is very important that you lie down or sit and are relaxed and well supported. You

Your baby could continue sucking on your breast even though he is finished feeding. He just really enjoys suckling. Beware that your baby is holding the nipple correctly. If not, your breasts could get irritated.

will have to experiment to find the right position for you. Ask a professional to help you the first few times if you can. You can put a pillow under the baby and your arm, or put your feet up if you are sitting.

Nursing lying down, Side lying

Nursing sitting, Cradle hold

Nursing sitting, Football hold

It is really important that your baby can breathe freely while taking the breast. Sometimes your breast can cover the nostrils. If that happens, gently pull the breast back from the baby's face. If your baby has a stuffy or blocked nose, use some saline drops from the pharmacy or ask the doctor for some nose drops to clear the way.

Starting to Nurse

If you sit or lie down comfortably, lay your baby horizontal on his side with your belly against his belly. If you're sitting, support his head with your wrist and underarm. If you want the baby higher or lower pull his bottom down a little. Point your nipple to the upper half of your baby's mouth. Touch your baby's upper lip with the nipple, the baby's mouth will open wide and quickly pull the baby towards you. Ease nipple and the pigmented area around it (areola) into the baby's mouth as his bottom lip curls to the

Your baby is in a good nursing position when:

His tummy lays against your tummy

The pigmented area around your nipple goes into the baby's mouth

His nose and chin touch your breast

His bottom lip curls outside

His bottom jaw moves up and down

His cheeks are round without dips

He swallows and you can hear it

The tongue is under the nipple

The mouth is wide open

outside. With the nipple safely in the back of the mouth, feeding shouldn't be painful. The baby will start suckling. For a while, the baby won't easily let go. While the baby starts sucking, the milk flow starts to go which is called 'let down'. Once in a while, the baby will take a little break and continue again until totally satisfied or wants the second breast. His needs for nutrition, sucking and body contact are satisfied this way. When finished, your baby will let go of the breast or fall asleep. Thank you, mommy!

'Let Down' Reflex

The 'let down' reflex allows the muscles around the milk glands to push the milk through the milk ducts. Not everyone feels this reflex very clearly, but you can always see it because there is milk in the mouth of the baby. This reflex works on both breasts. You will notice that your left breast might leak when your baby drinks on the right breast and vice versa. You can use breast pads that fit into your bra to protect your clothes from leaking milk. While feeding you can also use breast shells to collect the dripping milk. The first few days you may also feel this reflex in your uterus as it contracts while you breastfeed.

Nursing on Demand

Nursing on demand will help you get started with breastfeeding. If your baby is half awake and starts moving and making sounds you can pick him up. If your baby sleeps in your own bedroom (rooming in) you will have an easier time picking up on his signals.

It's much more productive for you and your baby to start nursing in a relaxed fashion rather than beginning as he is crying and in need of appeasement. The first few days you may be feeding your baby every one to two hours. A minimum of 8-12 feedings in 24 hours is recommended for the first few weeks. Soon you will develop an even rhythm and the frequency of feeds may decrease to two to four hours. Hopefully in the mornings he will sleep a little longer and in the afternoon and early evening he will want to feed more often and enjoy sitting with mommy. Most breastfed babies sleep uninterrupted for 5-6 hours during the night (until about 5 or 6 in the morning) when they are between eight and twelve weeks old.

How do you know if your baby is getting enough milk?

A baby that is getting enough will let you know when it is time for the next feeding. The baby is awake before feeding, feeds 8 to 12 times per 24 hours and is relaxed and satisfied after nursing. A baby that takes enough has (after the fourth day) a minimum of six wet diapers a day and a minimum of one stool. The stool is yellow and soft when you breastfeed. It is not unusual for a baby to have more than one of those diapers a day. And some babies have many. You will feel your breasts are relaxed after nursing. A baby that feeds enough grows. You can verify this by weighing your baby. The first few days after birth your baby loses weight, but from the fourth or fifth day the weight will gradually increase by about one ounce per day.

Within two weeks your baby should be back to his birth weight.

If you think your baby feeds too little then carefully watch how your baby feeds from your breast. Do you hear him swallow? Does the jaw move up and down? Do your breasts feel relaxed after nursing? Does the baby fall asleep too soon while nursing? Try to offer some more feedings and take good care of yourself. Getting enough rest, liquid and food are very important for you now. You can use a hand or electrical pump to express some extra milk after nursing to stimulate the milk glands and make more milk.

If you think your baby isn't gaining enough weight then go see your doctor or pediatrician. A certified lactation consultant can be of tremendous help in teaching how to breastfeed. Your doctor or midwife can refer you to such breastfeeding specialist. Or you can call La Leche League International at 1800 LALECHE or check online at www.lli.org. They can answer many of your questions.

Baby's Stools

During the first weeks your baby will have a dirty diaper a few times a day with thin, yellow bowel movement speckled with little seedy spots. After six weeks, the bowel movement can vary from a few times a day to once a week.

Engorgement

A few days after the delivery your breasts can feel painful and swollen because of engorgement. This develops because the body is sending more blood and fluids to your breasts. Moreover your milk production is increasing rapidly. You can prevent engorgement by breastfeeding your baby often the first few days and nights. As soon as the milk production is readjusted to the needs of your baby, the engorgement will disappear. Often this takes a few days. If you carefully position the baby at your breast, the normal 'let down' reflex will provide milk for your baby. You can stimulate this reflex by putting warm compresses on your breasts before feeding. Take enough time for feeding.

If your breasts are excruciatingly painful you can try to get some relief by:

- Using different positions during feeding which will releive the pressure just a little bit differently by emptying the breasts.

- Put a cold compress on your breasts after feeding, like a cold washcloth

Don't Panic

When you have nipple cracks, the baby could suck a little bit of blood during feeding. When the baby spits some of the milk back, there could be some blood in it. If blood in the mouth continues and you can't find a source of blood on your nipples, then see the pediatrician.

or the old-fashioned way with cold crushed kale leaves. Don't use kale method if you have nipple cracks.

- And if none of these provide relief, as a last resource you could pump your breasts empty one time, and if necessary, you can repeat that again.

Sometimes the 'let down' can be so severe that your baby isn't able to 'latch on.' The best thing you can do is to pump your breast a little bit first so that the nipple becomes a bit softer and the baby can try again. You can try manually expressing milk or using a hand or electrical pump.

Nipple Problems

When the nipple is flat or inverted, the baby may have a lot more trouble latching onto it. Still you can nurse your baby with a flat or withdrawn nipple. Massaging your nipple or pumping a little bit just before starting to nurse can make it easier for you and the baby. Ask a professional to help.

The first few days your nipples can be very sensitive. Try to inspire your baby as functionally and gently as possible. After a week, the nipples should be used to nursing and the sensitivity will decrease.

Nipple Cracks

Nipple cracks are little tears in the skin of the nipple. They can develop with improper latch, skin irritation, or thrush. The cracks are painful and make nursing very difficult. The cracks also increase the risk of getting a breast infection. If you are stressed and have pain then the 'let down' reflex won't work as effectively. The baby may get restless while nursing and let

loose more often or suck very hard.

How do you prevent nipple cracks?

Take the time to put your baby on the breast. Only put the baby towards your breast when his mouth is wide open leading the nipple to a safe place in his

Growth Spurt

Most of the time your breasts will produce enough milk for your baby. Sometimes the baby starts a growth spurt and will need more milk than you are making at that moment. Milk production could also decrease because you are sick, not getting enough rest, or are having your period. You'll notice this because your baby is suddenly very unhappy and wants to feed 'all the time'. Don't worry, no problem. The 'adjusting days' are the solution. On an adjusting day, you retract yourself from all your appointments and activities. Get comfortable on your bed or in a room with only your baby and enough food and drinks for yourself. Nurse your baby every two hours and allow him to drink as long as he wishes. The increase in nursing signals your body to produce more milk as your baby enters a growth spurt. Within a few days your milk supply should have increased and your baby will be satisfied and back on his normal nursing rhythm. Ask for and accept help with other responsibilities to free your time for feeding.

mouth. If it hurts then don't be afraid to take your baby off your breast and start over again. Breastfeeding should never hurt!

Wash your breast with water only and treat the skin around your nipple with care (never rub hard). You can leave a drop of milk on the nipple after feeding and allow it to dry. The milk protects the nipple against bacteria. You could also put a thin layer of nipple cream on your well-dried nipples. Discuss this with your doctor before starting. Change your nursing pads after each feeding and wash your hands regularly. If you do develop cracks, then start feeding with your least painful breast. If the milk starts flowing in both breasts you can change the baby to the painful breast. Offer your breast frequently and briefly and it is better not to take long breaks in between. Keep your nipples as dry as possible and 'air' them out regularly.

If the pain persists, then discuss with your doctor what you can do. For example, you could pump for a few days to give your breasts some relief. This has to be done at least six times a day. Try to use different feeding positions and you could wear a nipple guard in your bra preventing the nipple from touching anything.

Breast Infection (mastitis)

A breast infection mostly occurs in the period from the first week to six weeks post delivery. Although it can happen anytime, you are more predisposed to this if you are tired and have little resistance. Nipple cracks, a clogged milk duct or thrush can cause a breast infection. Get used to examining your breasts regularly, for example, while you are taking a shower. The first signs of a breast infection are hard painful spots in the breast, red breast skin and eventually a feeling as if you are having the flu with a temperature rise to about 101° F (38.4° C) if not higher.

In the case of a threatening breast infection it is very important to keep your breast warm with, for example, a warm, dry pad. Nurse often in different positions and from the infected breast first. During nursing you could softly massage around the tense spots towards the nipple. If this doesn't work to loosen the tissue while your baby is drinking then try to pump and do the same. Empty the breast often and completely until the hard spot is gone and you feel better again.

With mastitis you will have a fever (higher than 101° F (38.4° C). You may feel very sick, and your breast will be hard, red, and tender. It is best to stay in bed, drink a lot of water and continue feeding or pumping. Put warm pads on your breasts before nursing. If it is comfortable for you, you can try cooling your breast when they are empty. Contact your doctor if you have a breast infection! She will prescribe antibiotics. These will not harm the baby, and in this stage it is very important that you continue nursing because it will get worse if you stop. Oddly enough, nursing will relieve some of the pressure and make you feel quite a bit better. Within ten days after starting the antibiotics, if not sooner, most symptoms of the infection will be gone.

Pumping or Expressing Breast Milk

If your baby isn't able or doesn't want to feed from your breast, you can get the milk production going by expressing or pumping the breast milk. The baby can get the pumped milk with a spoon, cup or bottle until it is ready to feed from the breast itself. If you stop breastfeeding and pumping for any reason your milk will begin to dry up within a few days.

To pump effectively, it is very important that your breast milk starts flowing and you have a 'let down'. This can be stimulated by looking at a picture of your baby, resting, putting warm pads on your breasts or breast massage. Pump as much as you would nurse because that way the breasts are producing enough milk.

You can pump in different ways, by hand, with a hand pump or electrical

Tips

Give yourself time to get used to breastfeeding.

Nurse daily in different positions. This promotes emptying every part of the breast and prevents a preference position from your baby.

Alternate the first breast you offer at each feeding. To help remember which breast was used last, put a safety pin or ribbon on your bra.

Prevent nipple cracks.

Get enough rest, for yourself and during nursing.

Prevent draft or cold from getting to your breasts.

Wear clean, cotton and non-binding bras.

pump. You can also pump both breasts at the same time. It will save you time and increases milk production. With hand expressing, you massage the milk out of the breast (very useful in emergency situations). Take the breast in your hand, thumb on the top and fingers on the bottom and massage the milk carefully out of the nipple.

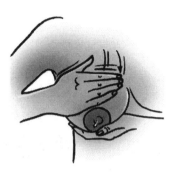

If pumping is difficult, you need help or if you want special recommendations you could consult a lactation consultant. Besides being a breastfeeding specialist, she also knows her way with pumping issues.

Mom's nutrition
Healthy and varied.

Drink extra water.

Eat three normal meals a day and a few nutritious snacks in between.

Eat fruits and vegetables, whole grain breads and cereals, calcium rich dairy products and protein rich foods (meat, fish).

Limit the amount of caffeine you are taking in.

Avoid alcohol and don't smoke around your baby.

Be very careful with medications. Consult your doctor first if you need any medication. Everything that you take in could end up in your breast milk, too.

Pumping

Pumps are available for purchase or rent. Don't be disappointed if you pump just a little bit of milk the first few times. Change breast side if the flow stops or diminishes. Repeat changing two to three times so that you will get as much milk as possible.

Wash your hands before touching anything and make sure all materials you use are sterilized by boiling them for a few minutes or use a special sanitizing device.

Label every container with the time and date you pumped the milk.

Storing Breast Milk

The breast milk can be kept at room temperature for about 6 to 8 hours at no warmer than 77°F. Refrigerated milk can be stored for up to three days and frozen breast milk can last longer (from 2 weeks in the freezer of your refrigerator to 6 months in a separate not-opened-so-often freezer/deep freezer). Do keep in mind that if you freeze the breast milk for 6 months, the composition of the milk will be different from the one your child needs at that moment. Never refreeze breast milk!

Thawing Breast Milk

To thaw breast milk you should never use a microwave. It can disturb the nutrients and the milk can be too hot for your baby. Thaw the bottle or container in warm water or leave it in the refrigerator overnight to allow it to defrost.

It is normal for the milk to separate into

milk and cream. Gently swirl the bottle to mix it before feeding. Do not stir or shake it. In addition, the breast milk may normally appear bluish, yellowish, or brownish. Some mothers report that it smells soapy. This is fine, but it should not smell sour.

Use the thawed breast milk immediately or keep it in the refrigerator for no more than 24 hours.

Formula Feeding

If breastfeeding doesn't work for you or should you not be able to do it because you are sick or have to get to work soon, and are unable to pump, then concentrate on giving your baby the best formula feeding you can. One of the benefits of formula feeding is that your partner can also feed the baby. Hold the baby close to you and talk with your baby while feeding. This way your baby gets used to your smell, feel and voice.

Preparing the Formula

Put everything you need on a clean kitchen towel. Work as hygienically as possible.

Wash your hands!

The formula is prepared one bottle at a time. Carefully follow the instructions on the formula's packaging. Improper mixing of formula is common and may harm the baby.

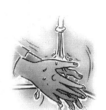

You can check the milk's temperature by putting a few drops on the inside of your wrist. The milk shouldn't feel too cold or too hot. Store the formula powder in a dry, cool spot.

Enough Milk for the Baby

Sometimes the baby won't drink as much as it normally does. Stop feeding if the baby isn't hungry anymore and throw away the remainder of the formula. A bottle-feeding will take about 15 to 30 minutes. If it takes the baby more time to empty the bottle, this could mean that the hole in the nipple is probably too small. If the baby empties the bottle in just a few minutes then chances are the hole in the nipple is too big. Do take into account that the baby can take more time one day and drink faster the next. And every baby has his own pace, be aware that if a feeding takes little time, the baby may cry because his sucking need wasn't satisfied. Get informed by a professional as to what a good feeding schedule for your baby would be, what kind of formula is best suited for your baby, and how much you need to give your baby. The first few weeks the baby needs to be fed every 2 to 4 hours. The first day most babies take less then one ounce. After the first few days, babies take 2-3 ounces per feed. The rest of the feeding schedule depends on you, the baby, the formula you are using, etc. Discuss this with someone who is educated in this field.

Bottle Nipples and Bottles

There is a wide variety of bottles and bottle nipples from which to choose. There are tapered bottles, waisted, easy grip and disposable bottles with liners. Most common nipples are the 'cherry' model (which looks like a nipple), the 'dental' model (which fits in the jaw of your baby), and the wide based nipple for disposable bottles.

What you should know about bottle nipples:

- Never use a nipple for more then six weeks. They are worn out by then.

- Store the nipple dry,

- Sanitize the nipple every day.

The bottle needs to be cleaned every time after use. You could use warm water and a special bottle cleaner, a uniquely designed steam unit that you can use in the microwave, or clean it in the dishwasher. The first few weeks it is necessary to sanitize the bottles by boiling them. Place the bottles in boiling water for at least 10 minutes and boil the nipples for 3 minutes.

Even though you are bottle feeding your child, the first few days after delivery your breasts will feel swollen and tender. Check your breasts daily.

1. Boiling water

2. Water in the bottle

3. Measure formula

4. Add the formula to the bottle of

5. Stir or shake

6. Check temperature

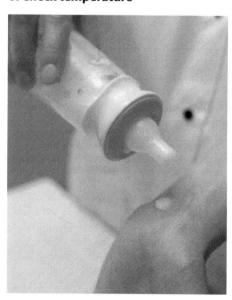

Boiling bottles (10 minutes)

Boiling nipples (3 minutes)

After 6 weeks throw away nipples

Burping

While the baby is drinking from the bottle he will also ingest some air. The baby will get rid of the air by burping after he's done drinking. It can take a while before the burp will come and sometimes it won't.

Stooling

After a few days of drinking from the bottle, the bowel movements will look the same every time. It is pretty firm and has a yellow-brown color. For a baby, cow's milk is a lot harder to digest than milk from the mother. That's why babies who are bottle fed sometimes have constipation problems. If such is the case, see your pediatrician. A bottle fed baby should have bowel movements at least once every two days.

Depending on the weight of your baby, your baby should get a bottle every 2 to 4 hours and will take 2 to 4 ounces each feed. Feed your baby on demand and let your baby decide when he is finished drinking. You don't have to finish every bottle entirely.

 It is important to change your position during feeding. This way you'll prevent your baby from developing a preference position. Check out the breastfeeding positions on page 50, which you can also use while feeding with a bottle.

Room for pictures :

Taking Care of your Baby

Changing a Diaper

Before you take the baby out of bed, prepare the changing table. Put out a clean diaper, wipes and baby ointment.

1. Open the attachment slips of the diaper and fold them so they don't stick anymore.

2. Clean the buttocks and groin. Always wipe from 'front to back' especially for girls.

Watch Out!
Never ever leave your baby alone on the changing table – not even for a second! Leave the phone and doorbell for a minute. Everything will have to wait. If it is really urgent then first put your baby back in his bed – even if diaper is half on.

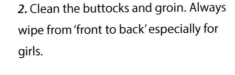

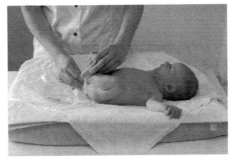

3. Fold the dirty diaper and toss it.

4. Slide the clean diaper under your baby's buttocks with the closing strips on the bottom.

5. Take the diaper and pull it in between the legs.

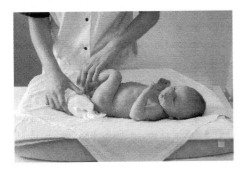

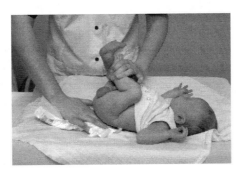

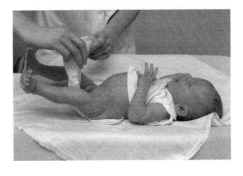

6. Fold the top of the diaper to the inside just under the bellybutton.

7. Let the diaper follow the curve of the belly.

8. Open the attachment slips and seal them on the diaper on top of the belly.

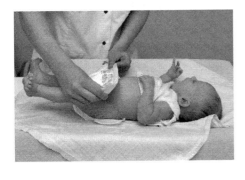

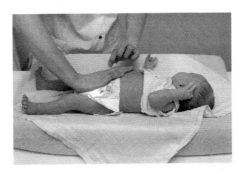

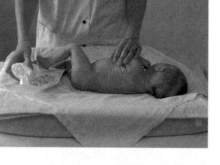

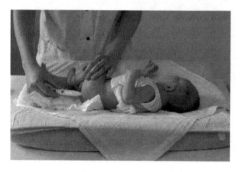

Use a right size diaper to avoid the risk of 'overflow' and spoiling those fabulous first clothes. Be aware that boys like to 'sprinkle' around just a second after you take off their diaper. And girls can do that too. Make sure to point everything down before closing a boy's diaper.

Taking Temperature

Cold hands don't say anything about the temperature of your baby. You don't have to take the temperature of a healthy baby. You can do a quick check by putting two fingers in the back of the baby's neck.

If the neck doesn't feel cold or too warm then your baby's temperature is probably okay. It is important that your own fingers feel normal if you check like that, so be sure they are not too cold or warm. If you have the feeling that the baby's neck feels too warm or cold, check the temperature with a thermometer.

In the first few days after delivery, taking the temperature should be done daily because it is important to check if the baby can keep his own temperature well.

For the first 3 months, any temperature of 100.4° F (38 °C) or greater needs to be seen by a doctor.

Prevent and soothe red, irritated bottoms. It is very important to avoid contact between the bottom and irritating fluids like urine and stool as much as possible. Changing diapers frequently and washing the baby's bottom with warm water should keep him clean and comfortable. Besides that, you can protect them by dabbing on a little bit of ointment with zinc oxide.

Bathing

Before you take the baby out of bed assess the room's temperature, 70-75°F is ideal. Set aside clean clothes, a new diaper, a towel, washcloth, cotton balls, thermometer (to check the water temperature), and a brush or comb if you'd like.

Fill the baby bath with warm water. Check the water temperature with your elbow (or the thermometer), usually between 90° F and 100° F. The water shouldn't feel too hot or cold on your elbow.

A naked baby cools down quickly so you may want to clean the ears and eyes before you undress. After that, clean the bottom and then further undress your baby.

Eyes

Use a moist cotton ball and sterilized water to clean your baby's eyes. Rub gently from the outside to the inside of the eye, always towards the nose. Use new, clean cotton ball for every turn.

Ears

It is enough to clean the outside edge and the skin behind the ears with a washcloth or cotton ball. Never ever use a cotton swab to clean the inside of the ear as you can push the earwax to the inside and risk injuring the eardrum.

Nails

Some babies have really long nails. They can hurt themselves with them. Don't cut them for the first 6 weeks. If the nails are really long and there is a little hook you can gently try to tear that hook off or you could use a small emery board.

In the Bath

Undress the rest of your baby. Carry your baby by using your left arm to rest the head on and your left hand to hold the arm of your baby. When the baby is in the bath you can use your right hand to wash.

In the Tummy Tub

Support the baby with your left hand behind the head and your right hand under the chin. After washing your baby, place your right hand under the bottom to lift the baby out of the water. This way the baby will be supported well.

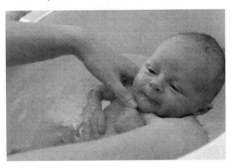

Getting Dressed

Thoroughly dry your baby after bathing him. Look at the pictures on the next page. Then pull the onesie over the head and after that pull the arms through the sleeves.

Wrong

Right

Neck Folds

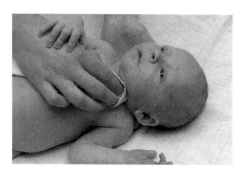

Knee Folds

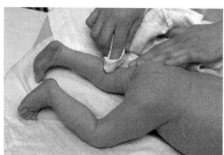

Onesie over the Head

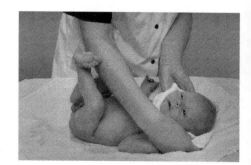

Armpits

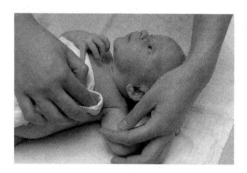

Buttock Seams

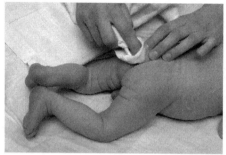

Arms in the Sleeves

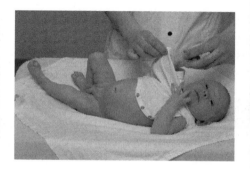

Neck Folds

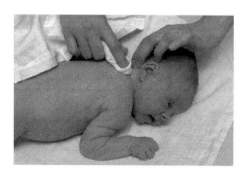

Groin Folds

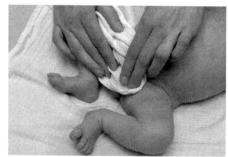

You don't have to bathe your baby every day. Washing with just water is the best for the baby's delicate skin as soap can be drying.

Delivery Report

Water broken   at _____ hour

Baby born   at _____ hour Date _____

Weight   _____ grams

Placenta _____   at _____ hour complete   yes   no

The New Mother

Episiotomy	yes	no
Sutures	yes	no
Medication	yes	no
Uterus contracted	yes	no
Urination after delivery	yes	no

Characteristics

_____

_____

_____

_____

_____

The Baby

Apgar score   0 1 minute   0 5 minutes   0 10 minutes

(breathing, skin color, muscle tone, reflex, heartbeat)

Umbilical cord	yes	no
Meconium	yes	no
Urine	yes	no
Presented breast within one hour after birth	yes	no
Feeding	yes	no
Temperature measured	yes	no
Vitamin K	yes	no

Characteristics

_____

_____

_____

Name Ob-Gyn/ Midwife _____

Delivery report made by _____

Additional Notes:

_____

_____

_____

_____

_____

_____

_____

_____

_____

_____

_____

_____

_____

_____

_____

_____

_____

_____

_____

Room for pictures :

Acknowledgements

As I was laying in bed at Saddleback Women's Hospital in Laguna Hills, California, checking things out in my Dutch version of this book, my pediatrician asked me what the book was about. When I told her, she said. "That would be a great thing for every new mother to have." But I was busy with my new baby and 18 month-old, so I didn't have time to get to it. A few years later I told my plan to translate this book to my Moms Club friend Melissa Sherman Pearl, who happens to be a great writer and editor. She encouraged me to just do it.

Well finally with their help, and that of a lot of other dedicated talents with big hearts and a sea of knowledge, the American version of the 'Kraamwijzer' is here.

Some pretty amazing women generously answered all of my questions. We discussed all that encompasses delivering and taking care of a baby in the USA, the politics surrounding this subject and they also found plenty of my mistakes in substance and in language matters. Kris Bagiu C.P.M., L.M. Midwife, Mona Saint M.D., M.P.H. of the Department of Obstetrics & Gynecology Hoag Women's Hospital Newport Beach, CA., Monique Dekker, director of Alle®zorg in The Netherlands, Maija Riikka Steenari M.D., Cynthia Jenkins and of course my editor-at-large Melissa Sherman Pearl. I so appreciated all of your help and dedication.

Also a big thanks to all my friends from the Moms Club of Laguna Niguel South, (especially those from Bunco), Geranda

Laros who made a beautiful cover photo and Yvanka and baby Sienna Betti for modeling, Jan Schrieber who did an outstanding graphic design job, Karin Erich and Kitty Seerden.

And last but never least, my husband Jan, my sons Nils and Tijn and my mom, for always giving me support and lots of hugs and kisses.

Gea

Index

Daily Observations

Use these daily observation charts to make notes every day about your feeding schedule and your baby's output. If you write down all of your observations every day, you can compare them with the previous days so you have an insight into the habits of your baby. And you don't forget it.

Time

In the 'time' section you can note the feeding times.

Type of feeding

Breastfeeding notes should include which side (a.k.a. which breast) you used and for how long, perhaps you switched sides mid-feed. Did you pump and then bottle feed? Did you use formula? How much did the baby drink?

Spitting up

If and how much did baby spit up?

Urine and bowel movement

What was in the diaper and how many diapers were there? This is to see if your baby is hydrated enough.

Remarks

Anything you would like to add that you don't want to forget.

Daily Observations Day 2

Time	Type of Feeding	Spitting Up	Urine	Bowel Movement	Remarks

Daily Observations Day 3

Time	Type of Feeding	Spitting Up	Urine	Bowel Movement	Remarks

Daily Observations Day 4

Time	Type of Feeding	Spitting Up	Urine	Bowel Movement	Remarks

Daily Observations Day 5

Time	Type of Feeding	Spitting Up	Urine	Bowel Movement	Remarks

Daily Observations Day 6

Time	Type of Feeding	Spitting Up	Urine	Bowel Movement	Remarks

Daily Observations Day 7

Time	Type of Feeding	Spitting Up	Urine	Bowel Movement	Remarks

Daily Observations Day 8

Time	Type of Feeding	Spitting Up	Urine	Bowel Movement	Remarks

Daily Observations Day 9

Time	Type of Feeding	Spitting Up	Urine	Bowel Movement	Remarks

Daily Observations Day 10

Time	Type of Feeding	Spitting Up	Urine	Bowel Movement	Remarks

Daily Observations Day 11

Time	Type of Feeding	Spitting Up	Urine	Bowel Movement	Remarks

Daily Observations Day 12

Time	Type of Feeding	Spitting Up	Urine	Bowel Movement	Remarks

Daily Observations Day 13

Time	Type of Feeding	Spitting Up	Urine	Bowel Movement	Remarks

Daily Observations Day 14

Time	Type of Feeding	Spitting Up	Urine	Bowel Movement	Remarks

Made in the USA
San Bernardino, CA
26 May 2018